SECRET ANGUISH:
My Mental Health Journey

By

Janis I. Soucie

ISBN: 978-0-359-38447-1

Dedication
To all those suffering from mental illness. I hear you! May your suffering be short and may you be guided and comforted by our great God as we travel on this rocky journey to better health

Table of Contents

CHAPTER ONE

It's March 11, 2018, a Sunday and I have been doing much thinking over my life as far as having mental illness goes. Over the past several years, a doctor diagnosed me with generalized anxiety disorder, depression, unspecified bipolar disorder, and borderline personality disorder. He also diagnosed with PTSD stemming from my father's own mood swings and emotional abuse.

This leaves me struggling to know where to go. There is a PTSD story that can stand on its own.

So where do I begin? Childhood? Somewhere in the middle? It's so tough to figure it out. I think perhaps I will start in childhood with my dad which means I'll be telling you about my PTSD story. Then I'll move on to the rest of my story.

God has done many wonderful things in my life. Perhaps one of the most amazing transformations I have seen was in my father. I was a little girl when I prayed for God's help with my Daddy and his moods. When I prayed I had no way of knowing what God was going to do.

My dad was a Christian man in his forties who had mud brown eyes, wore glasses and was going bald. He worked for Agway driving truck and delivering animal feed to various farms around New York state and into Canada. He was gone but he would come home for stretches at a time. He would often come home cranky.

At the time my two brothers, my older sister and I were the only kids living at home. My older two siblings were already married when I came along in 1981. So now we were in the mid-1980s when I was about three.

It was six o'clock at night and normally my father would be home. But my family and I ate dinner without him. My brothers and sisters went to their rooms and mother wandered off into the paneled sewing room to work on a current project.

I never understood why everyone went to their rooms every night. It seemed odd that no one stayed downstairs to watch TV or play board games together. They all went to their rooms and listened to their radios or cassette tapes. After a while, it became the norm, but I couldn't help but wonder about it.

Most of the lights downstairs were out. Only a lamp in the living room and one in the sewing room were on. I was a petite three-year-old with hazel eyes and long light brown hair. I wore one of my favorite dresses that my mother had made. I played with a doll in the living room, holding her close as I danced and sang in a soft tone.

Everything was right in my world and I was happy. I felt safe and content with my large family, even if I didn't understand them. I believed my family was sound, encouraging and happy. Oh, how I believed that with my whole childhood heart. I could never fathom anything different.

My mother, Betty, was a loving, caring and Godly woman, and did everything for her family. Her mornings began at 5:30. By 7 AM, after her husband had left for work and the kids were waiting outside for the bus, she sat in her favorite chair and read the Bible. She took a time-out for herself from chores around lunchtime. She ate, watched the noon news and her favorite soap opera, *The Young and the Restless*; she crocheted while she watched TV. After her break, she returned to her work. She vacuumed, did the dishes, cooked, baked, did the laundry, ironed the clothes, made the beds, and made sure everyone was on time for either school or work. She also made clothes for her children and their dolls. She was a typical homemaker. She was busy in the sewing room, her table lamp on, and sewing machine drumming away.

I loved it when my mother was sewing. I knew my mom was busy making something and it made me curious to see fabric sewn together. *What would the end result be this time?* There was also something comforting about the sound of the sewing machine. Mother was so great at making clothes for the four of us.

I listened to the sewing machine as I danced. I talked and sang to my doll in the dimly lit dining room. I twirled around and watched the hem of my dress spin out. I grinned and kept playing. I played my way into the dark dining room where I could see light from the paneled sewing room spilling in. My mother's sewing machine still clacking away.

3

A faint crying sound drifted into my ears. I stopped for a second, but didn't hear it again and continued to play. The sound came again. I stopped playing and listened.

But who was crying and why?

I thought of my two brothers who were upstairs in their rooms. But I could tell it wasn't them. Boys, cry? Come on now. They don't that, do they? I didn't think they did.

My sister popped into my head. Is Beth crying?

It sounded like a girl's cry. I listened harder and recognized the tone of voice. Mother! I never heard my mother cry before nor fathomed that she ever did. I was curious as to what made her cry. I walked calmly into the sewing room. There I saw my mother's face lit up by the light of the sewing machine and the light of the desk lamp. Her tears glistened as they streamed down her face.

"Mommy, what's wrong," I asked calmly and with great concern. I held my doll close for comfort.

"Your father's late from work again," she said through tears, keeping her light blue eyes on her work.

"Oh," I said and I walked away slowly and calmly, not knowing what to say or do. I wanted to comfort my mother but I didn't know-how. I was lost in thought and walked into the dining room.

All I could think was: *Daddy, why are you late? Why are you making Mommy cry? Daddy, if you're late 'again', then that means you have been late before. Why? What are you doing? Why are you not home with us?*

I went back to playing after these thoughts, but I wasn't as chipper as before. I felt something was wrong deep inside. I was deeply saddened.

Shortly after my father did come home but it was a stressful time. My other siblings questioned my father while he was in the kitchen having just come home. I heard my dad's upset voice and then he slammed the cellar door.

"Daddy, what's wrong," I asked walking toward him not afraid of his actions.

Mother looked down at me and said, "Daddy's upset. Go to your room. I'll take care of this."

I hesitated, wanting to help my mother and my father feel better, but Mother urged me to my room and so I went. I climbed the stairway to my room and left the door to my room open. This way the hallway light could shine like sun rays into my room. I could hear the commotion downstairs as I stood in my room still clutching my doll; I was not going to let her go. My tiny heart raced. I couldn't see what was happening and this made me uncertain. I realized I was afraid.

There was so much noise coming up through the register. I looked down through the register and could see the light was still on in the kitchen. I backed away as I remembered something important that my parents taught me. God. I had remembered what I had learned in church. I could always go to God with whatever was on my heart. So I did.

"God, my Daddy is so upset. Please, help him feel better. Help him to be a better person." I paused and felt something else I needed to say. "Whatever is hurting inside my Daddy, can you make him feel batter?" After I finished I felt God would take care of everything. I didn't have anything to worry about.

As I grew, I learned my family was not what I thought it was. It was not encouraging in the way I had imagined, nor was it "together" or happy. My father was moody and because of his uncertain moods, my brothers and sister often disappeared into their rooms. I didn't understand this at first I was still too young.

But there was a day when my dad, mom, my sister Beth and I went to church to clean it. It was a Saturday morning and the sun was shining. I was in a great mood. My sister was in cleaning one of the children's Sunday School rooms and my mom was out in the hallway dusting bookshelves. My dad was in the kitchen mopping the floor. I helped Beth for a little while before taking a break and then I went to help my mother. We were dusting down the books when I wondered what dad was up to. Mom, Beth, and I were all together and I felt bad that dad was alone. Maybe he was lonely. I jumped up and went into the kitchen. I stopped and looked at where I stood. I had stepped onto the wet floor. I quickly jumped back into the other room but not before my father saw me.

Even though it was an accident and I wanted to tell my dad I loved him, my dad was angry.

"Janis, I told everyone not to step into the kitchen. I aught to skin you alive."

I ran back to my mother and asked her what being "skinned alive" meant. She told me it meant removing my skin while I was still alive. I was so shocked by the explanation I don't remember saying anything. I do remember thinking, *"Would Daddy do that to me?"* I didn't have an answer.

I used my imagination and thought of what it would be like if Dad skinned me alive. The thought grossed me out and I shook it away. I wasn't going to bother dad when he was busy. I didn't think he would skin me alive, but it scared me anyway. I didn't know if he would do it or not. I made sure to stick with mom or Beth, mostly mom, the rest of the time we were cleaning.

This was the second time I remember being afraid of my dad. And it didn't stop there.

Concerning Sleep

I wasn't able to sleep well at his place. I was always uptight about everything that needed to be done. I hated how Dad complained I did chores wrong. Dad was always one to rush projects. He would have a fit over them when the projects weren't done in time or in the manner he wanted them carried out in. Between doing what he and others wanted, there wasn't much time for me to exercise, or do what I wanted. When everyone was asleep there was time for me to write-uninterrupted time-but by then I was too tired to write. This went on until I was too tired during the day. I would take a nap when Dad was outside doing yard work. I would always wait until he would be less likely to be able to figure I was sleeping. Because then I felt he would say something to the fact of, "how could you be so tired when you hardly did any 'work'." Well… work as far as he was concerned. He never did say anything but I felt guilty anyway.

Concerning the Shower

There were times Dad would be angry with me for taking so long in the shower. I would be in a shower about fifteen minutes and about another ten putting lotion on, getting dressed and brushing my hair. He is so darn impatient it seems longer! Even told him that too. I remember one time he even had me in tears and huddling under the covers of my bed over wanting to be clean and feel better about myself. He made me feel awful. Then he came to my room to apologize. He even said that he did the same thing with Mom. Didn't exactly make me feel better, but made me feel sorry for my mother and wonder more of what he put her through. Though, I accepted his apology I knew it was shallow. I knew he'd do it again.

Concerning the Phone

I always felt I had to be in a different room to speak to anyone. I never wanted Dad to find out too much about me. Not sure why other than it was a way for me to protect myself. Rightly so though. Every time I had finished something I was proud of he would criticize it instead of appreciating it and see it for what it was. He was like with all of us though. He's so unappreciative and always has been. Sometimes he's said he was proud or appreciative, but I've always wondered either way. Even in December, he kept being on my case about talking with Kevin for so long on the phone. Come on! I'm twenty-three! I'm not a child though he still treats me like one. Yet, he said nothing when I would talk with Heather or Kelly for hours.

Movies or music

He always had something to say about things I would watch or listen to. This made me want to be alone even more as well as the following:

Support

Especially with writing. He told me I'd be lucky to have a book published by the time I die. Gee, thanks, Dad. This makes me miss Mom even more. She enjoyed reading what I would write.

Being around my dad, even watching a movie with him, made me uptight. I wanted desperately to go to my room and work on my own hobby. This was rooted in childhood when he'd be moody. The sad part is, now that I'm out of the house I still feel like I should be rushing around even though I don't have to. Still can't help to notice how different, perhaps relaxed I am, compared to how it was back at the house. Now trying to train my brain to chill out is another issue. With all these doctor's appointments and new opportunities, I feel like I'm in a rush again. That's what I don't want. I want to chill my body out and take things slowly. Hard to do when your body is getting used to all the changes. I mean I can relax and able to sleep well. I could take naps when I feel the need and without guilt. (This part of feeling on a rush could have been hypomania and anxiety, but I wouldn't have known that then.)

Cleaning

My mother taught me many ways to clean the house such as dusting, vacuuming, doing dishes, and laundry. After her death, my dad kept telling me how he did household chores like my way of doing the wasn't enough. He started expecting me to do chores or gardening his way. I felt like the way I did chores were no longer good enough. Again, I couldn't just be myself. I felt like I had to be someone else to please him. When was he ever going to accept me for who I was?

After that, I had scattered memories. I only recalled learning to stay away from my dad when he was home for fear of making him angry. He was so easily upset most of the time. Meals, snacks, and desserts were catered to him.

It was hard to learn that my father was catered to and I couldn't have "his" special treats. Even though they were some of my favorite snacks. This made me feel less worthy and less important. I wondered if my mother did this to try to make him happy, so he wouldn't get upset so much. I don't know. But I can tell you when that pivotal moment came where I realized something was wrong in my family.

CHAPTER TWO

One evening, I was playing in the dining room. This room was near to the living room where Dad, Mom, and Alex were watching "Wheel of Fortune" and "Jeopardy". I was laughing and enjoying myself as a kid does when they're having fun with their toys. Then suddenly I heard, "Janis will you shut up!" The first time I heard this I just shrugged my shoulders and went back to playing though quietly.

I was a little older when I heard that line come again after I had been laughing at something my niece had said. I quickly grew quiet and thought, *Okay, sorry. I was just laughing. I don't see what's wrong with that. Why is it never okay to be me?*

After that moment, I became sad, quiet, and selectively mute. I felt that no matter what I said, Dad would either tell me to shut up or criticize something I said. So what was the point of talking?

I didn't feel comfortable in my own home. Something wasn't right. I had a great fear of my father already. Could I be even more afraid of him? I hoped not.

I became so afraid of him I struggled to be in the same room with him. I held my breath hoping he wouldn't notice me and I was tense. I was alert to where my exits were and I would feel the urge to flee the room. I just could not be near him and be comfortable. Not like a daughter should be able to do. (As you can see I had an awful time with anxiety here.)

I didn't even get a break when I went to bed. My dad's room was right next to mine. I had a squeaky daybed so every time I moved it made noise. I was so afraid to move for fear my father would yell at me for making too much noise.

So living with a moody father, where you had to cater to him to stay on his "good" side, was horrible. I never knew when he was going to blow up at everyone. Or when I was the only child living with him, I would get the brunt of his moods. The blow-ups were bad enough but grew worse after my mother died leaving me to fend against my father alone. Well, I wasn't alone and I prayed all the time. If it weren't for God's help, I know I wouldn't have gotten through that mess.

When my mother was alive, she was my safety net between my father and I. I felt I could go to her with my troubles. If I needed to ask Dad a question I would ask her if she could ask him for me. I was that afraid of him. His moods were so uncertain I was scared to find out which mood he was in. This kept me from talking to him and getting to know him like a daughter should be able to do.

In January of 1999, my mother was feeling ill and throwing up bile. She went to the emergency room where her temperature spiked. The doctor ran some tests and they found that her gallbladder was packed with gallstones. They did surgery to remove her gallbladder, but also found tumors in her stomach. They were cancerous. She had a rare form of ovarian cancer. In February, she went through cancer surgery. She tried chemotherapy but reacted to the antibiotic they gave her before chemotherapy could even begin. It was at that point she decided not to undergo chemotherapy. I was seventeen when this took place and I had to care for my mother until she passed away on April 8th.

My safety net was gone, and I felt left behind, vulnerable to whatever may happen next. I felt thrown into a nightmare.

I turned to poetry and lyric writing as well as praying and crying to get my emotions out. I felt I had no one to talk to. I couldn't talk to my dad. My sister Beth had started work now that her youngest was in school, so it was hard to get a hold of her. I felt alone but in writing, I found solace, a peace, which I didn't know writing could bring.

Without my mother, I had to deal with my father by myself. I tried to talk to him but all I would hear back was, "I'm sorry I'm such a bad father," even though I never said anything like that. I got so frustrated trying to talk to him.

And when he caught me crying because I missed my mother he would say, "You should be out with your friends missing your mother." It didn't make much sense to me, but I think I know what he was trying to say, is that I should be out with my friends more. He didn't bother to comfort me himself. Maybe he didn't know-how. I'm not sure.

My family never came together to talk about my mother's death and how we each were doing. I could have used that support, but it wasn't there. So I dealt with my mother's death through writing and staying in prayer.

But nothing could have prepared me for what I would have to face without having my mother to turn to for support. My niece Jessica is two years younger than I am and she had many people in her circle. I was around nineteen when she came into my room with three teenage guys. She left suddenly telling me she would be outside by the bonfire. I was astonished she left the guys in my room. I was nervous and not outgoing like she was. The guys eventually got bored and wanted to go back outside to be with Jessica so they left. It was such a relief to have them out of my room, but I was still angry with my niece.

That evening when my dad came home from work at Wal-Mart I told him about my niece bringing three guys up to my room. I thought he would be furious and protect me. Instead, he said, "Why didn't you go for it?"

This came from a man who was a Christian and taught me to wait until I was married for sex. My mind spun, my heart sank, *Just what exactly do you think of me? I can't believe you would tell me to do such an act and not protect me from this.*

I don't remember what I said to him. I was so awestruck and deeply hurt by his words I just went to my room. The belief that my father would protect me decreased, and I felt I knew what he thought of me by his comment.

But it only got worse. My dad used Paltalk a lot to connect with other people around the world. He often was in a singing chat room and probably others. I don't know for certain because I was never in there when he was on the computer. I felt like he'd yell at me if I was, so I stayed away. I knew about the singing room because I could hear them. Dad always had the speakers turned up when in that room.

I'm not sure what room he was in when he met Ryan. Ryan was an epileptic, but also on probation for something he did. My dad never told me what he did but he brought this man from Canada into our home and introduced him to the family. I was twenty at this time. Dad allowed Ryan to stay at the house for a month or so at a time and it first started during the winter months. We lived in an old farmhouse and the upstairs wasn't heated. We used electric heaters, but on windy days they did no-good. I could feel the cold wind come through the bedroom walls. It was a windy night when Dad asked me if I was okay with Ryan sleeping in his room on the floor; the guest bedroom was too cold. I didn't want this guy to freeze, but at the same time, I thought it an odd question.

My blankets curled under me and I was warm, the TV was on in the background. I looked up at my dad dumbfounded and shaking. Something inside me wanted to say no like something bad was going to happen, but I was still afraid of my dad. So I said, "Okay. So long as he sleeps on the floor."

I listened to them talking and dad moving Ryan's belongings into his room and then I heard not one, but two people crawl into my father's bed. I screamed inside. I longed for someone to talk to but felt I had no one.

But there I was alone in my bed, knowing my father was in bed with another man. I was just praying nothing sexual would happen. The knots in my stomach made me feel sick. What was happening to my family? It was like once mom passed away, everything else was falling apart.

I was hoping that my dad sharing the bed with Ryan was all that was going to happen. I was so wrong. Throughout the month that he stayed with us, Ryan took many photos of me and I didn't understand why. Then he started showing me pictures of naked celebrities. I don't know what he thought would happen but I wasn't interested. Then he started doing the house chores like laundry and suddenly my underwear came up missing. Since I knew Ryan had done the laundry, I confronted him about my underwear and I got it back. I threw them right in the trash! I was so upset that this had happened to me and that I had to throw my favorite pairs of underwear away.

I also babysat for my niece. She just had a little boy named Kevin and took care of him since he was born. There were times when Kevin was asleep, I would slip away and take a quick shower. When I got out and went to check on Kevin I found him gone. Ryan had taken him upstairs in the computer room. I suddenly hear Kevin cry and Ryan tells him, "It'll be alright." And then Kevin's wailing again. My heart raced and I feared Ryan was hurting Kevin in a sexual way. This turned my stomach. Ryan came downstairs like nothing had happened and I took Kevin back. My niece and her boyfriend took Kevin home.

The next day she asked me to babysit again and I told her I would. But she also told me there was blood in Kevin's diaper when they went to change it the night before. I told Jessica what happened. She saw I was upset and she comforted me and reassured me that she didn't blame me. I was extra vigilant as I could be that day, but I had to go to the bathroom. Once Kevin was asleep I ran to the bathroom and tried to be as quick as possible. I came out to find that Kevin was gone again. I yelled for Ryan throughout the house and couldn't find him. My heart pounded fiercely and my mind was circling with thoughts. Where could they be?

Why has my father left me alone with this guy? Why isn't he protecting me? Doesn't he care about me?

I walked outside into the backyard where I found Ryan holding Kevin on the bench swing. I walked up to Ryan and said,

"Ryan, you can't just take Kevin like that. I'm babysitting him and I need to know where he is. Please, stop taking him without my knowledge."

Ryan didn't take him again after that but he still kept an eye on Kevin.

I talked with my sister-in-law on the phone when she called a while later and told her everything. She was doing a background check on Ryan. She found out he was a pedophile and Dad was not to leave him home with anyone under twenty-one. I just happened to be twenty when Dad would go to work and leave me with Ryan. When I learned what a pedophile was I was scared.

The next day, my sister Beth called and said that she had talked with our sister-in-law and found out that Ryan was taking my underwear. She wanted to know if it was true. I told her it was but that I had confronted Ryan and got them back and threw them in the trash. I didn't want to know if he had done anything with them.

"Are you going to tell dad what's going on?" Beth asked.

"No."

"Why not?"

"Because he's not going to do anything about it."

"Well, if you're not going to tell him, then I will."

And she did.

That night, when Dad came home from Wal-Mart, he sat down on the bench seat in the dining room and called me in. "Why didn't you tell me Ryan was taking your underwear?" he asked.

"Because I got them back and didn't see that you would do anything else."

"I'll have a talk with him," he said and went upstairs where Ryan was in the computer room.

Did things change after that? I was hoping they would. I was hoping my dad would take Ryan home and have nothing more to do with him. But that's not what happened. They continued to see each other. Sometimes Ryan would be staying with us. And then there were times my dad would travel to Canada and stay with Ryan. I loved it when dad stayed over at Ryan's. That meant I was free from having to be front and center from the crap that was going on. I felt safe when they were gone.

There was one day Dad was back on the computer and he was talking with Ryan through Yahoo Messenger at this point. I was downstairs in the living room with recipes all over the table. I was trying to organize them and I found several recipes from Ryan. I saw parts of their conversations they would have through Yahoo Messenger. My body shook with emotion when I read Ryan's words, "I can't wait to make love to you again."

I put the papers down and ran for the scissors. I cut out those parts of conversations I found and dumped them in the trash. Tears welled in my eyes. How could this all be happening?

I thought of my mother. I desperately wanted to run into the living room where I usually found her in her blue chair, crocheting. I wanted to sit and talk with her about Ryan. If she were there with me she would be able to take action and send Ryan home. If she were here with me, none of this would have happened. Dad wouldn't have dared bring a man in the house for sexual purposes with Mom still around. But Mom did know of Dad's doubled-sided love life. She had written a note in her jewelry box, that said that Dad had told her he was bisexual and even listed his male partners. So Ryan wasn't the first. And there was at least one other man on the list that I knew from church. I was so sick to my stomach with all of this and so stressed out and scared to death. I wanted this to end, but it was clear my father wasn't going to take that action.

Then one day, to my relief, Border Patrol came to our door and took Ryan away. They gave my dad a warning. If he visited Ryan he was never to take him out of Canada again because he wasn't to leave on the count of his probation. They also said that if they see him in Canada with Ryan in the van trying to cross the border into New York, they would arrest Dad. They threw me when they said they could arrest me because I didn't answer the back door when they knocked. But who knocks at the back door? I was suspicious and that's why I didn't answer the door. I felt it was for my own safety, but they had their reasons for going to the back door first, just in case Ryan tried to flee.

And that's where that ended, except in my mind I still had the memories and in my body, the emotions of everything I had been through. I lost trust in my dad to protect me. That's what dads are supposed to do; protect their precious daughters. But mine didn't. I felt he didn't care enough to want to protect me. He put me in harm's way where sexual acts could have happened to me. I'm so thankful nothing like that happened.

That is how I felt my life crumbled after my mother's death. I had a sense of loss of safety, trust, respect, and love. All the trust I found in my mother, I lost when it came to my father.

Losing my mother made me feel afraid, vulnerable, lost, uncertain, confused, and alone.

But my father...

I love him. It's not that I don't. But he hurt with his actions. As I look back, I wonder if he had a mental illness like bipolar with his so many ups and downs in mood. I wondered this because I know mental illness runs in the family. Yes, I have unspecified bipolar disorder with psychosis, PTSD, generalized anxiety disorder, and borderline personality disorder. Mental illness would explain his shifty moods and the way he would lash out with his anger at us.

Throughout all that I dealt with my father and all the times I wanted to run away, I stayed home. I don't know why other than there was something brewing inside my little body. My tiny heart kept believing in God and trusting Him to answer the prayer I prayed that one night. I never forgot the prayer and recited it all through my childhood and adolescence, even into adulthood. I knew God could work inside my father and change him for the better. I had no doubts. But I was yet to see the work God would do.

When I grew up and was out on my own with my own family, I talked with my dad on the phone. We talked about some of the past. I had gotten the nerve up to ask my dad about the criticism he always gave whenever we'd try to do something. I asked him if he meant the criticism to help us and he said yes, though it may not have come out that way. He wanted us kids to strive to be better, but he had a hard time showing it.

Hold it! My dad and I were speaking about the past? That right there is progress. Before my father would never talk about it. God was working with my Dad! How exciting and that I'm seeing the result of these changes. I felt blessed. But I'm not done.

My father not only spoke about the past but he also apologized for it! My heart melted as I heard the sincerity in my father's voice. Inside I was laughing at a teacher I had for a PTSD class who said that those who create the PTSD environment will never apologize for it. Well, I don't think that statement is accurate because my father *did* apologize.

That was the day that God healed the connection between my father and I. This happened in 2012 and it is now 2019 and my dad and I still have a great relationship.

I still have stuff I have to work through because of my dad's moods. But I know God is working with me on that and I have made some great progress. I know the progress I've made was only possible through God's intervention.

God worked with both my dad and I. He brought us to where we would have our relationship back and better than ever.

God never forgets! Nope! Not ever. He knows what you're going through no matter how tough or how simple the situation. God is right there to help you with it. Let God into your life and just see what changes He can make for you. All changes to work for your good and prosper you because He is a loving God and wants the best for all His children.

CHAPTER THREE

Now that I have told you my PTSD story I can go on with the rest, but we will have to go back in time a bit. In 2003, I was talking with my best friend, Heather. I told her I felt God was telling me life was going to be challenging for me for a while. In the end, it would be better than I could imagine. She asked me what I meant, but all I could tell her was that I felt life was going to go negatively for a while before getting better.

The following year in July I started not to feel well. I believe it was because I was physically dealing with symptoms that came from a psychological origin. You see, to escape my dad's moods I always ran to movies, to writing, or books to get away because I couldn't "get away" otherwise. I became so engrossed with escaping I was living in these other worlds and my own reality and emotions associated with it were numbed, if even recognized. I got used to being zoned out, but something happened that made me realize my life was going nowhere and I wanted a change. With coming out of my daydreams I saw my reality and was feeling the anxiety from my situation. I was feeling so sick with an upset stomach and emotions that were on the high. I cried a lot but wasn't fully understanding why at the time. My stomach hurt and I struggled to eat anything.

It got so bad I went to the Emergency Room but all they told me was that I was stressed out and had nausea. (Later, in 2015, the doctor found a large gallstone that had been there for a while. So this was a contributing issue to my abdominal pain and why I struggled with nausea and keeping food down back in 2004.)

After being told stress was causing all of my issues, I thought of the subjects in my life that might have any contribution. When I stopped and thought about all aspects of my life that might be stressing me out, I couldn't place anything in particular. Perhaps, the only thing that I wished could change was that I could be more energetic than other people and feel up to getting out more and doing more things. I didn't dwell on that and living a low-key life felt normal to me as I had been living that way all of my life. Still, I felt like there was something agitating me, but was it external stressors? I didn't think so. How about physical? I couldn't think of anything physical going on with me that would cause stressful reactions within my body. What about emotional factors? Now there was something I had an idea about.

I did know I struggled with living in the same house my mother died in. After she died, my body often shook if I went downstairs at night to go to the bathroom because I thought I might see Mother's spirit, or hear her voice. I trembled still living in the house where I had memories of taking care of Mother and then her passing. I couldn't take it then and I desperately wanted to move. Yet I was not ready to be out on my own and I knew I had to continue to live my dad and I knew he wouldn't move. Living daily with the memories and environmental reminders of everything I went through while taking care of my mother wore on me and I had to find a way to handle it every day. I pushed memories out of my mind and refused to deal with them. That was the wrong thing to do, yet I didn't know how else to handle the situation. Perhaps the area concerning my mother was causing stress in my body I was not aware of.

Then there was the issue of growing up with a father who, on viewing him, didn't know how to show affection. He was critical and gave a few compliments. He rarely, if ever gave support apart from financial. He had mood swings, everything had to be done his way or it wasn't done right. Although your way of doing chores still got the job done. He cheated on my mother and made her cry. I even saw him hit her once when she wouldn't stop crying because she was scared we weren't going to financially survive.

I know I was always scared of my father and could never talk to him let alone be in the same room with him for fear of upsetting him. I'm sure having dealt with this all of my life that this must have had some negative effect on me.

There were at least two health events I remember happening in early October of 2004, just after my twenty-third birthday. I had been feeling rather well most of the day compared to how I had been feeling in previous days. Then by early evening, I was feeling horrible again with anxiety, crying and feeling so cold that I had the shivers and my teeth were chattering. My body was trying so hard to get warm that my muscles were tense and aching. I found Dad and told him how I felt. He had me lay down on the couch and he covered me with a blanket. I still couldn't get warm and he went upstairs to get extra blankets and his electric blanket. He put the electric blanket on top of the one blanket I already had on, plugged the electric blanket in and turned it on. Then he placed at least one more blanket on top of the electric blanket. I was already wearing pants, heavy socks, a T-shirt, a sweatshirt, and a heavy jacket. I was still crying and my teeth were chattering, trying to tell Dad I didn't know what was wrong. He told me a couple of times to stop crying and I did as best I could. He said he would make me some soup and see if that helped. I was grateful he decided to help me that much, but I think I fell asleep before I even got the soup. The warmth of the blankets gradually warmed me up and relaxed me enough to get some shuteye.

A few days later, I was laying on the couch in the living room still not feeling well. I was cold, exhausted, and I couldn't breathe well. I felt like someone was sitting on my chest. I shut my eyes and tried to get some rest. However, I would wake up gasping, trying to catch my breath. This scared me and anxiety kicked in as well as did the crying. I called for Dad and he walked into the living room and asked me what was wrong. I told him I couldn't breathe. He looked at me and said in a frustrated tone, "Jan, I don't know what's wrong with you!" He stormed out of the room and I was left alone and scared. With my mother gone, I didn't have anyone who was patient enough to tend to me, to comfort me, to talk to me and help me figure out what was going on. Dealing with something like that alone increased my anxiety. All I wanted was someone to hold me and help me through what I was going through. However, I had no such comfort or support. I desperately wanted my mother back!

October 26, 2004, was the next "big event" I had recorded. I wasn't feeling well and complained of terrible stomach pain that felt like my stomach was tied in knots so tight they could never be undone. I would often hold my stomach or rub it to try to make it feel better. When I thought that anxiety might be causing the stomach upset and pain, I approached my Dad and asked him what the Bible said about anxiety. He sat down at the dining room table with me and opened the Bible. He read various verses and while he was reading, I felt myself relax and I felt good hearing the Word of God. I always felt this way when Dad would read the Bible to me, but it was when he stopped reading that I became aware of the stomach pain again. I started to cry because it hurt so bad and curled up on the dining room floor in terrible pain. Dad walked into the side room, or paneled room, to the phone, and called a doctor. He said I had something wrong with my stomach. I don't know all that was said, but Dad said he was going to take me to see a doctor.

I pulled myself to my feet and realized I was freezing. I was so cold my teeth were chattering and I was shivering. Dad grabbed a blanket and ushered me outside to his Dodge Caravan. I hopped into the passenger seat and he handed me the blanket. He started the van and then went next door to get my sister Margie.

Dad was comfortable with Margie being with us as she had a bout of anxiety and depression when she was younger and Dad thought she might be able to help me. Even though the doctors in the ER said I was stressed and anxious, I felt there was something else horribly wrong that was overlooked.

A few minutes later, Margie followed Dad to the van. Dad climbed behind the wheel and Margie climbed through the side door and sat behind me. Dad and Margie talked about where to take me and it was decided we should try a health facility on Washington Street, which connected to the road we lived on. The place we tried was fairly new, but I had no luck getting in to see a doctor. The next place we tried was North Country Urgent Care out on Coffeen Street. Margie and Dad went up to the front desk while I took a seat in the waiting area. They relayed my complaints to the woman behind the counter and she was able to get me in to see the doctor.

After fifteen minutes or so of suffering from stomach pain and emotional unrest in the waiting room, I was finally called in to see the doctor. I followed the nurse, a tall light-haired woman, down the hall and took a right into a small room. I climbed onto the padded table while Margie and Dad filed into the room behind me. They sat in two chairs to my right that were against the wall. The nurse took my pulse and found it to be slightly fast. My temperature was then taken and it was over one hundred degrees. The nurse finished with the rest of my vitals and left the room saying the doctor would be with me shortly.

I don't know how long I waited but it seemed like forever. I feared what would happen if the doctor didn't come soon. I thought I might go crazy. I needed someone to figure out what was wrong. Someone who could help me stop shaking, ease my tense, painful muscles, calm my stomach, bring my temperature down, and clear the fogginess out of my brain. I needed help fast because I could no longer handle being so sick.

I looked over at Margie and Dad and wondered what they must think of me. Even though I wondered, I didn't want to ask. I feared to know their thoughts as I felt they might be negative toward me. I didn't know why I felt this way and quickly pushed it out of my mind.

The doctor finally walked in. He was tall, thin with dark hair. He asked me how I felt and told him about my symptoms. He checked my throat and ears and listened to my heart and lungs. Everything must have seemed normal to him because he didn't say anything otherwise.

Margie stepped in and mentioned something about me not fully getting over my mother's death. This set the stage for the doctor to take a different approach with me. I wasn't sure what to say to the doctor at first. Before he walked in I didn't have anything on my mind, yet my body was still trembling, my heart was racing and I was scared of what might be wrong. After what Margie said about me not getting over my mother's death, I couldn't help but think that very well might be the case. I knew still living where she died was bothering me.

It was difficult to remember everything that I said when I felt like I was stuck inside a dream with a thick fog swirling around in my brain.

However, enough was said on the matter to warrant the doctor's diagnosis of depression and anxiety. The doctor prescribed Wellbutrin XL, which I was familiar with by way of frequent TV commercials. After the diagnosis was ruled, he said the nurse would return with the prescription and he left the room. (All this time there was no check on my gallbladder, which I know was causing me problems. Nope! I was dealing strictly with mental illness.

I felt better having talked to a doctor and knowing I was going to be given something that would help me feel better. I felt a minor release of anxiety and tension after the talk with the doctor, though worry crept back in when Margie mentioned her concern over the prescription I was given. She told me she knew someone who was put on Wellbutrin XL and the woman bounced off the walls. I wasn't looking to bounce off the walls. I had a hard enough time trying to relax enough to rest. I thought I would try the drug anyway and see what happened.

The nurse came in a few minutes later and handed me the prescription. She talked a bit about the drug and made sure I understood the directions before allowing me to leave. With the prescription in hand and Margie and Dad behind me, I followed the nurse down the hall, through a door, and into the waiting room. Margie, Dad and I left Urgent Care and drove to Wal*Mart on Arsenal Street to get my prescription filled. We then went home.

Shortly after arriving home, Dad called a couple of our friends, Pastor Dan and MayAnn who were starting up a church on The Square in Watertown. Dad talked to Pastor Dan about me, which led to Pastor Dan and his wife MayAnn, to drive to our house. I can't remember what the whole visit entailed, but I remember the part where Pastor Dan spoke with Dad saying I didn't need the medicine I was prescribed.

In my heart, I knew Pastor Dan was right. I didn't even want to take the medicine because there was no way to know how it would affect me, whether for better or worse. I didn't know what to do other than to follow the doctor's directions, yet I felt I kept being misdiagnosed.

After Pastor Dan and MayAnn left, I talked to Dad and told him I believed what Pastor Dan said. I told him I didn't think I needed the medication. He said okay and didn't press me to take any more than the one dose I had already taken when I came home. He knew eventually that it was my decision.

CHAPTER FOUR

October 29, 2004, was a day I'll never forget. The events were the second scariest I believe I had ever dealt with until that point. The day was cool but sunny and I was feeling good. I was up and about in a happy mood and decided to work more on painting my room, which I had started the day before. I made a small lunch of a sandwich and a drink. After lunch, I went upstairs, put on old painting clothes, and worked on painting my room a pale peach color. Within a few minutes of painting, I felt a change within my body I could not explain. I started not to feel good but pressed on a little longer. I continued to paint and my thoughts wandered from thoughts of my future to curious wonders about family and friends and how they were doing.

Suddenly, I felt so sick I could no longer paint. I felt sick to my stomach; I was crying; my head hurt and I felt all jittery were I couldn't relax, sit still or concentrate. I felt like I was running from something by being constantly busy, and by stopping, whatever I was running from, would catch up with me. More than likely I was dealing with anxiety. I wasn't sure if the paint fumes that were making me so ill, or I was still in the house where my mother died and where my father still roamed.

Crying and shaking uncontrollably, I put the paint away, went downstairs and frantically searched for the Wellbutrin XL. I was beginning to think I needed the medication, but when I couldn't find it, I lost it. I started getting anxious.

I called my sister Margie and through sobs, I told her how I felt and that I couldn't find my prescription. She calmed me down and said she had some relaxants and asked me if I wanted to try one. I was so desperate to calm down I didn't care what she had so long as it relaxed me. I told her that I wanted to try the relaxant and that I would be over in a few minutes.

I hung up the phone but before I went over to Margie's, I went into the bathroom and took an Alleve to help ease painful menstrual cramps. I then went over to Margie's and she gave me a relaxant. I curled up on her couch under a blanket and watched TV. I was vaguely aware of my niece Jessica, nephew Matt, brother Matt, and his wife being there. I became so drowsy and relaxed it felt like everything was moving slowly, but I was content to be physically, mentally, and emotionally calm.

I dozed off on Margie's couch. I don't know for how long but the sun was gradually setting lower in the sky. I decided I had better head back home. Dad would be home in a few hours and I hadn't left a note about where I was. Also, I wanted some peace.

Back home, I wandered half asleep, into the living room, curled up under a blanket on the plush blue sofa, and fell asleep. About a half-hour passed when the phone rang. I staggered over to the phone and looked at the caller I.D. that displayed the name of a neighbor from down the street. The only time this neighbor called was to let us know that Margie's horses were out of the pasture.

Margie had always owned horses since before I was born. They were her source of pride. I loved her horses as well and didn't want anything to happen to them. I hung up the phone, tossed the blanket back on the couch, and in a zombie-like daze, I sauntered over to Margie's trailer. I slowly walked up the wooden stairs, through the door and stepped inside.

Margie was sitting on the couch holding her twin granddaughters—my great-nieces—Emily and Lauren when I told her that our neighbor from down the street called and said the horses were out. Margie noticed what I said, though she couldn't personally do anything about the situation. She was busy babysitting so she couldn't catch the horses. She did mention sending Matt, her youngest, to go after them. I said okay. I turned to leave and head back home when I felt intense nausea in my stomach and strange light-headedness. Everything started to go black. I said, "Oh, crap," and bent my knees to lower myself to the floor when I collapsed.

Time was lost to me before I started to hear voices though they were faint. I couldn't bring myself back so I laid there, my body feeling like a deadweight, and listened to what was going on around me.

I felt Margie grab my arms when her daughter Jessica walked in the door holding her son Kevin. The door banged against my leg as Jessica walked in and pushed her way inside. Jessica asked what happened, Margie told her what I said just before I collapsed and that I hit my head on the shoe rack on the way to the floor.

I heard Kevin's two-year-old voice cry out, "Aunt Jan! Aunt Jan!" and he started to cry when I didn't respond.

Jessica opened the door and yelled to my brother Alex that I had passed out. Alex didn't seem too concerned and thought I would come around eventually.

Margie had Jessica grab my legs and they managed enough muscle strength to haul me over to the couch. The events that happened after that seemed sketchy for a bit as I kept feeling like I was drifting away, but would return to a certain conscious level.

I believe Margie called Dad to see what he wanted to do. I knew Dad was at work and I thought he would be furious with me for being called home. I didn't know if this would be the case or not, but that was how I felt. I heard Margie say Dad was coming home and to call 911. Margie must have made the phone call to 911 but I really don't remember much about that. I must have drifted then.

The next I heard were sirens in the distance, growing quickly closer, then footsteps on the stairs and strange voices drifting through the door and to my side. Everything seemed so mottled to me with so many voices, but I caught, "What happened?" which was followed by an explanation.

I felt rubber hands on my body; the paramedics were checking my vitals. While they were doing so, I believe it was Margie who mentioned I had started a new drug. This led to the paramedics wondering if I had overdosed. I think Margie sent Jessica next door to my house to look for the medication. She came back with a frantic tone when she couldn't find the Wellbutrin.

Dad must have shown up at one point and they asked him where the medication was. I think he left with Jessica to go find it and returned with the medication sometime later. Margie and Jessica counted the Wellbutrin caplets and found the only tablet missing was the one pill I had taken the day I received the prescription. They all realized I hadn't overdosed.

By this time, the paramedics ruled my vitals to be normal. Yet, I didn't feel normal. I felt I was in limbo, barely here barely there. Suddenly I became ice cold and started shaking, my body doing what it could to warm itself.

I heard a male voice say my name and tell me that if I didn't come to they would have to put a tube down my throat and put me on oxygen. When that didn't work, I felt a few sets of fingers pinch the insides of my left thigh and call my name. That did it! The reoccurring pain from the pinches was enough to bring me back completely. I opened my eyes to find at least six people staring down at me. With the golden rays of the setting sun filtering into the room, in combination with my foggy brain, it all just seemed like a bad dream. I could see things but it felt like they weren't real. Even emotionally, I felt removed from the situation. I was numb to what had happened and not yet completely coherent.

My family was relieved to see I was awake, but I could tell by the looks on their faces they were genuinely concerned. I looked at the paramedics and recognized a couple of faces from Sackets Harbor School. The first was female and was my former bus driver Bonnie. Another was a young man with light hair and blue eyes by the name of Kenny who was at least a grade ahead of me. The other paramedic was an older man I didn't recognize. The men helped me down the stairs and outside onto a gurney.

On the gurney, I thought I recognized the man standing by the back entrance to the Guilfoyle ambulance as Doug, also a bus driver at Sackets Harbor School. With all of these familiar faces, I realized how embarrassed I felt and just how real the situation was.

The paramedics loaded me into the ambulance and Dad asked if he could ride along. He was told no. Dad asked if someone would call Pastor Dan and someone said they would.

After that, the doors of the ambulance were shut on my family and I was enclosed in the steel box on wheels with a strange man, and Bonnie, a familiar face. I was sympathetic toward Bonnie having lost a daughter, one of my classmates, a year before. Remembering this made me think of my dad and I wondered what he must have been feeling.

Bonnie asked me why I had stopped taking my medication. I told her I didn't know. She told me I should keep taking it as it would make me feel better. I nodded and resigned myself to the fact that I would have to take the medication.

The trip to the hospital's ER entrance was rather short only about ten minutes if that. I lived on the same road as the hospital. Inside the bright walled ER, I was transferred to an ER gurney and wheeled to a room that was only separated from other sections by curtains. I waited there by myself for a while before anyone came to see me.

I don't remember the whole ER stay. Accept there were many tests run on me like a check of alcohol in my blood, pregnancy, as well as the salicylate and acetaminophen levels, which are pain killers. ECG tracing, a complete blood count with a few other tests were also performed. After all of that, I was released a few hours later with the diagnosis of a mood disorder and possible or fainting. However, what I think happened was the Aleve I took for menstrual cramps and the relaxant Margie gave me were incompatible which caused the drop in blood pressure and therefore fainting.

November 30, 2004, was the day I started seeing a regular doctor. My dad drove me to Clayton to my doctor's office. My doctor was tall, thin, young, and handsome. He was also married. I was told he was Christian, which made me more comfortable about seeing him and more apt to trust him.

I talked to the doctor though I can't quite recall the conversation. I do remember mentioning my concern over a racing heart and the possibility of thyroid problems as I knew they ran in my family. The doctor said he would do some blood tests and see how everything came out. We would then go from there. I agreed with this plan. The doctor left and a nurse came in and took samples of my blood. She left and I sat alone in the plain cream-colored room for my results to come back. I was happy to be getting my results so soon as the blood tests could be done right there in the office.

Finally, the doctor came in with my results and told me everything came back fine. My thyroid test came back normal though it was on the high-end. I didn't know what that meant and never thought to ask. A cardiac risk panel to check for the risk of heart problems was run and that too came back normal. I was at a loss and frankly so was the doctor.

I don't remember the rest of the visit well save for more conversation about my life and previous Urgent Care and ER visits. Again, I was diagnosed as depressed and put on Prozac.

CHAPTER FIVE

December 6, 2004, marked another landing in the ER of the Samaritan Medical Center. I had an intense throbbing headache, sharp pain in my stomach, burning pain in my chest. The pain in my stomach was so severe I would double over in tears. My headache was so bad light and sound bothered me and I couldn't concentrate on anything.

After a long wait, I was called back into the ER and my dad went with me. Vitals were taken which again were normal. The doctor talked to me about things going on in my life and suggested bringing a social worker in. I was nervous at this and not sure what bringing in a social worker meant.

A female social worker with long, dark, curly hair had Dad leave so we could talk in private. I wasn't entirely sure what to say to the social worker. I just knew that I didn't want to go home because I didn't feel good there. What I meant by that I didn't fully understand, but I was adamant about not going home. I'm sure the social worker may have secretly thought the reason I didn't "feel good" and didn't want to return home was perhaps due to my father. I don't know for sure but I didn't ask. I know part of the reason I didn't feel well at home was because of anxiety and doubt about my life.

After our conversation, the social worker said I could either admit myself to the hospital's mental health unit, or they would admit me. If I admitted myself, I would be able to leave when I wanted. If they admitted me, I would be in the mental health unit until the doctors decided it was appropriate to release me. I signed myself in, not wanting to go back home where I wouldn't feel any better. To be honest I wasn't afraid to admit myself. I felt a peace about it like being there I could the help I needed.

The social worker left and a few minutes later, a wheelchair was rolled over to me. Wearing a hospital gown, and trying to keep the back of it closed, I climbed into the ominous wheelchair that would take me someplace I thought I would never go. The social worker pushed me to a place I had only seen in movies. Mental institutions were always large and filled with people you would swear were possessed. I had all of these dark, freaky images in my head and had to shake them away before I freaked out.

An orderly pushed me through the ER to an elevator. Dad followed us as we climbed onto the elevator. I think we rode the elevator up to about the fourth floor and then got off. I was calm this whole time even as I was inched down the cream-colored hallway, drawing ever closer to the Inpatient Mental Health Unit. We stopped at one door, and the orderly opened it, wheeled me through, and stopped again in front of another door. Sandwiched between two doors, in a small plain cubicle, I had to say good-bye to my father.

I felt a few things now I didn't understand. I was calm but why the calmness overcame me suddenly when I had been previously uneasy didn't make sense. Was it because I was going to be away from home and whatever was making me sick? Was the calmness because I knew doctors would surround me so that if anything happened, I would be taken care of?

I wanted to cry as Dad and I said our goodbyes. I looked into his tearing brown eyes and knew he was hurting over what was happening with me. I knew then he cared more for me than he could otherwise express. I felt genuine concern and love and wished there was something I could do to comfort him. Yet, something was going on with me, only I didn't understand just what was happening.

I said good-bye to my dad and gave him a hug before he left and headed back toward the elevator. I sat in the wheelchair with a brown paper bag in my lap, which contained my clothes and shoes I had worn to the hospital. I stared at the door in front of me trying to picture what lay beyond it. I watched the orderly in front of me push a button on a contraption on the wall by the door. I wasn't sure what this did, but I guessed it connected him with someone on the other side who had control of the door.

When we were buzzed through the door, I was pushed down a short hallway with rooms on both sides of me. At the end of the hall was the nurse's station where we stopped. The orderly handed over my clothes to the nurse and my clothes were checked. I was nervous while my clothes were being looked through. I had no idea why it had to be done. After the nurses were through, my clothes were given back to me save for my sneakers. I was told my sneakers were being kept in a locker for me because a suicidal might try to get a hold of the laces. At least then I understood why my clothes were searched and relaxed about the whole thing.

The orderly then wheeled me back down the hall and pushed me into a room on the left. He dropped me off and then left. I quickly changed into my clothes and sat down on my bed. Shortly after, a male doctor in a white coat sat next to me at a dark wood table to my left. He asked me all sorts of questions though I don't remember the conversation very well. I do remember him writing down much of what I said while I sobbed. I think I may have brought up my Mom's passing this time around but I'm not sure.

The next morning I was awakened at six by a knock and a voice at the door. I wasn't sure what was going on but I scrambled out of bed and groggily shuffled to the end of the hall in front of the nurses' station. There were two lines forming there with a nurse at the front of each. I learned quickly by watching others that we were getting our blood pressure, pulse and temperature checked.

We were allowed to go back to bed until breakfast came around eight. Breakfast was brought up to our floor each morning and was available until ten. Showers were also available, however, there were about four stalls to the women's shower room. I was shy about other women seeing my body so I took a shower when I was sure no one else was in the room. Each day there was a daily schedule of activities that I had yet to learn. I didn't feel like doing much of anything so I slept through whatever may have gone on that morning.

When I did get dressed and up for the day, I complained of not being able to calm down. I felt jittery like something was bothering me. I was given Klonopin, which calmed me down so much it knocked me out. I don't know how long I was out for but my doctor, a tall, dark-haired man, came into my room to talk to me. He sat at the desk beside my bed and asked me why I was asleep. I told him about the medication I was given and how it made me so drowsy I couldn't stay awake. He told me the medication was too strong and he would have the dosage lowered. He postponed our conversation and thankfully let me sleep.

I believe it may have been the next day, December 7, 2004, when this doctor called on me again. This time I was taken into a room, down the hall, with a desk against one wall and two chairs facing opposite each other. I took the chair next to the desk while the doctor sat at the desk with my file opened to its contents.

Pen ready in hand, the doctor asked me what sorts of things were on my mind that brought me to the hospital. At first, I struggled with what to say. I really didn't feel like there was much bothering me. I may have briefly mentioned Mom's passing but if I did, I didn't focus on her. I didn't feel her passing was my main struggle. There was something else that remained elusive.

I talked with the doctor for ten or fifteen minutes, though I thought it odd he didn't have any comments for me. He took notes more than anything and I was very curious about what he was writing about the conversation. By the time the session with him was over I felt more at ease and confident that he would help me.

Later, during one of the group meetings, I met a young woman with dirty blond hair and glasses named Melissa Shaw. We instantly became friends. It felt good and made me happy to have a friend on the inside. She helped to fill a void within me that came from feeling alone like somehow I was drifting from my family into a world unknown and without friends.

I had visitors every night between the hours of 7-8:30 PM. My visitors were my brother Alex, Dad, Pastor Dan and Sam. Sam was a friend of Pastor Dan's, who I had met back in October. I looked forward to visiting hours, though I was tense and uncertain when Dad was there.

The rest of my stay was quite a blur.

Release day from Inpatient Mental Health arrived on December 10, 2004. When I learned of my release, I had great anxiety. I was shaking and crying, highly fearful of going home because I thought I would only get severely sick again. Regardless of how I felt, I was given prescriptions for Zomig for migraine headaches, Klonopin for anxiety, Trazodone to help me sleep and Prozac for depression. I was then sent home.

December 10-24, 2004, my health did not improve. I still wasn't sleeping because my breathing wasn't right. I was crying and had a very upset stomach. Dad gave me two Tylenol PM to help me sleep and I slept downstairs in his plush blue recliner. Sleeping in his recliner at an incline helped me to breathe better. With the incline of the recliner and with the help of the Tylenol PM I was able to get much-needed rest. However, when I woke up, I started crying. I wanted to stay asleep and not face feelings of illness. I didn't want to deal with the fact I was back home when I so wanted to be away.

When I would wake up, dad handed me two more Tylenol PM. I wondered if it was safe to keep taking the medication as often as I was. I was feeling so awful I took the blue and white pills from my Dad, swallowed them, and soon was back to sleep.

I didn't eat much during this time due to a severely aching and nauseous stomach. There was a time I did remember getting hungry and asked my dad for something to eat. He offered to make me oatmeal and I agreed. A few minutes later, he returned with a steaming bowl of oatmeal with brown sugar and milk, the way we both like to eat it.

I ate the oatmeal savoring the sweet taste of the brown sugar. When I was finished, I settled back into the recliner and closed my eyes to try to get more sleep. Wave after wave of intense nausea hit and I headed to the bathroom to be safe. Nausea subsided a bit and I thought I would be all right and my stomach was reacting to being empty for so long. I used the bathroom figuring I may as well since I was there. I washed my hands and started to feel sick again. I threw up in the sink. I cried while I cleaned the sink out and then brushed my teeth. I wasn't feeling good; I was exhausted and I was worried about what might be so wrong with me.

Later, of the period from the 10-14 of December, I had a good day and decided to go out. I went over to Bill and Cris's house who were friends from the church I went to located on The Square in Watertown called The Beacon of Light Christian Ministry Center. Also at Bill and Cris's was Cris's daughter Alicia and Pastor Dan's friend, Sam. Sam and I spent an hour or so snowmobiling in the fields around the house. I felt so happy! I loved snowmobiling. There was always something about flying over snow while riding on a machine of power. I was the happiest I had been in quite some time.

After snowmobiling, Sam and I went inside crawled out of our snow clothes and got ready to eat dinner. The five of us piled our plates with food and then went into the living room to watch a football game as Bill and Cris's favorite team was playing. When I was finished with dinner and my dishes are taken care of, I laid down on one of the two couches. Sam had the couch opposite me; Alicia was on the floor and Bill and Cris were behind us in their own recliners.

We enjoyed the game but after about ten minutes, I forgot about the television. My stomach started cramping. I was moaning from the pain and when the stomach pain grew worse, I broke out crying. Sam looked at me wondering what was wrong, but it was Cris who came to my side. She asked me what was wrong and I told her I didn't feel well and that my stomach hurt badly. I felt very warm like I was running a fever. I thought for sure my body was still fighting something but I didn't know what. If it was a bug, I couldn't seem to shake it and had been fighting it since July. I couldn't help but feel I was fighting something else. (This could have been a gallbladder flare up.)

Cris put a cold, folded washcloth on my head to help cool me down. I felt awful and anxiety over what could be wrong continued to grow. Cris asked me if I wanted her to call dad and see what he wanted her to do. I told her yes. When she hung up the phone, Cris said they were going to take me home. We piled into their van and I was sprawled out in the backseat in the fetal position. The pain in my stomach was bad and I couldn't stop crying.

We stopped at a convenience store and Cris bought me Pepcid AC hoping it would help calm my stomach. I took a tablet praying that it would work faster than what the box said which was that it could take a full week for the medicine to fully work. The next stop we made was home. Bill and Cris helped me into the house and into the living room where I laid back down on the couch. The longer I was home the worse I felt. Cris took my temperature and she said I was burning up. My stomach still hurt bad and I was clenching my teeth and crying hysterically.

Dad called Samaritan Medical Center not knowing what else to do. He spoke with a doctor there and told him the symptoms I was having. The doctor then wanted to speak with me. I calmed my sobbing as much as I could and took the phone from Dad. The doctor flat-out said that all I was dealing with was anxiety and when it gets bad it can feel like I was dying. I do not remember much else from the conversation because I was furious with the doctor. Everyone kept diagnosing me with depression and anxiety, yet when I did everything they said to help me "get better", nothing changed. I still felt so sick it was interrupting my life. Something else was going on but the doctors weren't listening to me.

On December 25, 2004, at 3:48 PM, I made another trip to the ER. My vitals were taken and I saw a doctor. Again, I was diagnosed with general anxiety disorder. I was crying continuously and was put in a room by myself. Dad and my sister Margie were there with me. Pastor Dan and my Aunt Art, one of my Dad's sisters, were called and they arrived sometime later.

I was curled up on the bed and crying. I wanted my mother and wished she hadn't died five years earlier. Mother always knew how to make me feel better. At my mentioning of Mom, Margie suggested that I hadn't dealt with my mom's passing. I felt I had dealt with her passing, but I feared I might be wrong in my judgment.

I complained of difficulty breathing and mentioned this to the doctor when he came in. He gave me a gown to put on and everyone stepped out of the room while I did so. Minutes later, I was in a wheelchair being pushed down the hall into an x-ray room. X-rays were taken of my chest but they came back normal. I was relieved in a sense but not in another. If the x-rays were fine, why was I having a hard time breathing?

I was taken back to the room, where I changed back into my clothes. My medications were refilled and I was discharged at 8:45 PM.

Five days later on the thirtieth, I was back in the ER. Vitals were taken and before long, a social worker was sent in. I talked with the social worker and this time brought up my mother's passing in case Margie might have been right in my not fully dealing with the grief. I was asked if I wanted to admit myself to the Inpatient Mental Health or be admitted. I again admitted myself.

Back in the mental health ward, I went back to the routine of having to get up at six in the morning to have my vitals taken. At times, my pulse was over one hundred and my temperature was one hundred and one. A nurse asked me if I felt all right but I told her I didn't and went back to bed.

There was one day I had layers of clothing on including my fleece bathrobe, socks and slippers, pants and a few shirts, but I was still freezing. My teeth were chattering and I was crying because I couldn't get warm. I sat out in the hall on the floor crying. One female patient asked me what was wrong and I told her I was cold. A doctor passed by me and asked the same question. I told him I was freezing and he simply told me it was just my nerves and walked away. He didn't help me feel any better. I was more frustrated by his lack of help on the matter.

The day came to talk to my doctor just as I did the last time I was there. I had the same tall, dark-haired doctor as before and we sat in the same small room. I was in a cushioned chair facing him as I talked. I talked about my mom's passing but he didn't have much to say on this matter.

I brought up the concern my doctor in Clayton, NY and I had about sleep apnea. I was also still crying because of frustration as well as physical, emotional, and mental exhaustion. My doctor responded to me by saying, "People with sleep apnea are tired. They don't cry." This made me angry. He didn't know me at all and made assumptions about those with sleep apnea. When I get overtired from not sleeping well, I get nauseous, have more anxiety and I cry as a result. After the session was over, I never wanted to talk to the doctor again let along pass him in the hall. (Later in 2016, I was found to have sleep apnea.)

Through my time in the mental ward, I noticed how my health was better. I wasn't getting as sick as I was at my Dad's. I knew something back home had to have been making severely ill, but I had no idea what the culprit could be. (My dad had the roof of the old farmhouse repaired and a lot of black dust sifted into the house. I was feeling sick since then.)

Saturday, January, 1st

Can you believe it? Here I am on the second floor in the Mental Health Ward at Samaritan Medical Center, spending the first day of the New Year. Never had I imagined I would be spending a New Year's Day in a place like this. All I could think about was how everyone else's New Year's Day was a lot better than mine. Yet, in all actuality where I am isn't so bad. I'm away from so many things that bothered me.

In my quiet time, I thought of what I wanted to do with my life. I wasn't sure if I wanted to continue chasing a career in writing or take a different route. The same day I was considering my career choice, one of my favorite counselors called me into the art room. She was short, had short dark hair, and was young and kind. We sat at the art room table and chatted about a few things such as the next step to take in my life.

By then, the counselors knew I refused to go home and live with my father again. I knew something there was making me sick physically. I also knew mentally I could go back. The counselor and I knew I needed to go somewhere when I got out of the hospital and she said she could see what she could do so I wouldn't have to go home.

I even told her I had decided to quit writing and had even thrown out some of my work. She asked me why and I told her I didn't think my work was good enough. Her response was one I'll never forget: "If all the writers in the world threw out everything they had ever written because they thought it wasn't good enough, there wouldn't be anything left for the rest of us to read."

Her words struck me and I realized she had a valid point. I decided to reconsider writing as a career. The time I spent alone in Mental Health, was a time of self-reflection and gaining a closer relationship with God. I prayed more often than not for guidance in my life and where I should go next. I knew I was not to go home.

Later, in my room, I talked with a thin, blond-haired woman who spoke to me about Transitional Living Services. TLS is a program for the mentally ill who are given their own apartment to help them become independent. I told the woman I wanted to go into the program. I simply refused to go home and I wouldn't let them make me.

Friday, January, 7th

Last day in the mental health ward at Samaritan Medical Center. Two women from North Country Transitional Living showed up. One was oriental with long dark hair and the Japanese features; the other was short, with long thin brown hair. Her name was Alicia. They took me to Kinney's so I could fill out my prescriptions and then if I remember right, they drove me to Dad's house where I gathered some clothes and other personal items like bathroom necessities. They took me back to the apartment and help me unload everything. Then we went over some paperwork, some of it I had to sign. That pretty much concluded the day.

After the trip to Dad's, the women showed me my new apartment at 528 Franklin St, Apt C, Watertown, NY 13601.

When you first enter the apartment there is the kitchen with the sink to your left and the refrigerator and stove to your right; a dinner table sat in the middle of the kitchen. From the doorway to your immediate left, was a bedroom and a bathroom. If you walk through the kitchen there is a small living room with a couch, a coffee table, and two chairs. Through the living room and on the other side of a set of curtained French doors was my bedroom. I got to choose as I was the first one to move into this newly renovated apartment. And also because I didn't smoke and I was the first one to move in, it was a non-smoking apartment.

Thursday, February, 3rd

So many things have been bothering me lately. I've been frustrated by trying to figure out what's making me feel so unstable and I think, by the grace of God, I have found the source.

For so many years I have felt little worth to anyone save for my mom when she was still on the physical plane. I think I can pinpoint the incident that caused me to feel that way, besides causing me to withdraw from guys or go and hide whenever dad and mom would invite someone over, a military guy or guys, Martin, in particular. I wouldn't even eat at dinner time with them. I have been uncomfortable around guys and find it hard to be in their presence very long, yet deep inside I wanted a serious relationship. I had even begun to feel like there is a guy just around another corner waiting to either molest me or rape me. It's no wonder I don't' want to be alone when I go out because I don't want guys coming up to me. If they look at me I can deal so long as I don't really know about it. I'm even afraid to be alone in my own apartment, which I have been in almost a month, even when God is watching over me and the doors are locked. I still am edgy that some guys would break-in. Because Rodger molested me when I was three my life was changed from a perspective that affected my life greatly. Because of what happened I have a hard time being me. I like to be out roaming the shops on the square or even working at the church but there are guys all around. I'm not saying they would do anything but then there are those on drugs and alcohol who cannot be trusted. And then from Rodger who I totally forgot about until 5th grade when he came over but was not allowed to come near me and I didn't know why. I was about ten then and had forgotten what had happened to me. They told him not to go near me because I had fifth's disease and it was contagious. He still made the attempt to get near me but was told again to stay away. I think I may have asked why but I don't remember the answer I received. That was the last I ever saw of him.

Years went on and I gained weight for no seemingly apparent reason and I found myself secluded in my room more often than just when Dad came home angry from work. I easily went over 200 pounds with what Rodger did, how Dad acted and still acts (or has a lack of compassion and understanding) and how Matt and Gary would pick on me; Matt called me fat once. Then with all of the other male friends moving away, abruptly stopped writing letters after mentioning another girl (Martin) and then Josh saying we could be more if he didn't have to move back to Georgia and then Dustin who moved way too fast for a fifteen-year-old in a boyfriend/girlfriend relationship. And then there was Jim who totally used me and even made me paranoid.

I just want to be loved deeply and cared deeply for by a protective, caring and understanding man. Yet I am afraid to fall in love. I want to be really close to him, even get married and have a family, but then I have a hard time getting close to him and even loving him as deeply as I want to.

So far, because of what's happened, I have felt like I'm not worth much, anything I do has little or no value. I'm afraid to be alone because I'm afraid a guy will try to approach me or kidnap me and make me damaged goods before I meet the right man. Many have given me compliments that I'm pretty, beautiful, "you could be a model", but I just don't see it, or don't feel it is what I should say. Yeah, I think I'm pretty and I thank God for my looks but at the same time, I know guys are attracted to a pretty face and a slim body. I haven't had true, deep, honest love from anyone in a grand long time. Maybe it's because I haven't allowed myself to feel and accept their love because I don't feel good enough to be loved because I have been taken advantage of. I mean, what will Pastor Dan, MayAnn and Sam think of me when they find out? Or even anyone from TLS? When am I ever gonna feel love and worth again? Do these things still exist for someone like me? Yes. Through Jesus.

But being molested or traumatized at such a young age is having profound effects on my life now. I don't feel I can trust Dad or any of his friends especially Ryan!

I feel like a little kid even though I'm twenty-three. If I wasn't so emotionally distraught I'd probably be crying over this right now.

Secret Anguish: My Mental Health Journey

Dad and Heather haven't helped my writing career any. There again I feel like my writing isn't worth crap even though I know it has meaning because God granted me the gift of creativity. But by being molested I became shy and still find it really hard to get close to people. Men in general. Just don't feel like I matter too awfully much. But how could someone tainted be worth something to anyone? Only God knows that answer.

Still, I wonder how I'm going to handle tonight when I go shopping with MayAnn, Pastor Dan and Sam. Don't know how I will keep silent. Maybe when they call to pick me up I will see if we will be going back to their house for a little while. Think I will more than likely talk with MayAnn before I let Pastor Dan and Sam know. This definitely won't be easy.

Also another adage here! I didn't remember the molestation until after Mom passed away. One traumatic event triggered flashbacks of another. I thought they were fleeting thoughts or dreams at first until I told them to Becky. She told me they weren't dreams but that everything I said really happened. I remember it clear as day like it just happened.

The rest of February dealt with various appointments at Mercy Behavioral Health for medicine checks as well as initial appointments with a therapist.

43

CHAPTER SIX

March 8 and 10th, I had appointments with my therapist and with another doctor who checked my medications.

April 6th, I had an appointment with my doctor in Clayton at my request. I learned a couple of weeks earlier that I would be working at The North Watertown Cemetery and I wanted to talk to my doctor and address the allergy situation. I believe that is when he put me on Allegra.

Later that April, I was lonely in my apartment and rarely seeing friends began to get to me. I sat at my kitchen table, my laptop open in front of me. I decided to try a dating site but I was going to avoid sites like Match.com, E-harmony.com, and Cupid.com. I tried those sites but never had much luck. I decided to try a Christian dating site and searched on Google. One of the sites I found was MeetChristians.com. I went to the site, clicked on the sign-up link and sat there, staring at the sign-up form. I was feeling hopeless and didn't know if I could handle this sort of thing again. Before signing up, I prayed to God and asked Him if signing up for this site was really what He wanted me to do. If so, I would do it. I had a strong feeling to go ahead with the sign-up like somehow this time would be different.

Within two weeks, I met a man named Aaron and we started chatting by e-mail. I felt very strongly that this man was special. I had a wonderful feeling about where we were headed, but I knew I had to wait and see where God would take us. Having someone like Aaron to talk to made me happy and gave me an extra boost to get out of bed in the morning. He gave me something to look forward to.

April 28th, I started work at the office of The North Watertown Cemetery and would be working there, in the office, every week until Labor Day when the cemetery closed.

On May 10th, I had an appointment with my new therapist at Mercy Behavioral Health. My old therapist was leaving. I told my therapist about my impacted teeth and she was sympathetic toward me. I also talked to her about possibly getting Tea Cup, my Chihuahua that has been living with my Dad, to live with me. She said she did not see why Tea Cup could not live with me. She said she would have to talk to one of my other doctor's and she would get back to me. I had hoped my little dog would be able to stay with me. I knew at my dad's she was left alone a lot and had been misbehaving since I left. I did everything for her and I knew she was out of sorts. I was too and I knew getting her to live with me would make us both happy. I just needed the doctor's approval.

May 13th, Aaron called me again. We have been chatting on the phone for the past few weeks and I was happy with how well the relationship was going. On the twenty-first, we had a date and he was going to visit me so we could see the last Star Wars movie together. It was so easy to talk to Aaron and we would often talk for hours at night before we said good night. We were very comfortable with each other. We both knew God's hand was on our relationship and that He had answered our prayers of loneliness by bringing Aaron and I together. Talking to Aaron helped me forget how awful I was feeling and not many people could do that. May 21st, was the first day I met Aaron in front of the Best Western on Washington Street. He was more gorgeous in person and there was chemistry between us. We had a busy but wonderful day. We walked through The Square to The Crystal Restaurant for lunch. That was also where our first kiss happened. Then we cruised through a few shops such as the Agape Shoppe and the Second Look Bookstore before Aaron said he wanted to see where I worked. It was a walk but we walked out of The Square, down a side street, over the Court Street Bridge and took a left onto another street. We took a right on a side street and The North Watertown Cemetery came into view on our left. The office was closed so I was not able to show it to him. We walked over to the gazebo and sat inside it for a while until we got too cold and it started to rain. We walked back to my apartment and watched *The Little Mermaid*. I could not help but think how Ariel had her Prince Eric and now I had mine. We left about 6:30 PM to go to the Salmon Run Mall and Melissa Shaw went with us. We all enjoyed *Star Wars Episode III*. It was about 9:20 PM by the time we got out of the movie and had dinner at Wendy's there in the food court. Then Aaron drove Melissa home and then me. Aaron and I had a hard time parting ways. We so enjoyed each other's company and could not believe we had finally found each other. It took us a while but we were able to say good night, knowing we would see each other in the morning.

May 22nd, was a good day. Toward evening, however, things started to go sour. I was up early with thoughts of Aaron and the day we were going to have together. I showered and dressed and Aaron called. He was up early too and could not wait to see me. He arrived at my apartment shortly after 9 AM and we talked about what we wanted to do for breakfast. While we were chatting, my dad called. He knew Aaron was visiting and wanted to meet him. Dad asked if we wanted to go out to the house for breakfast. I asked Aaron if he wanted to meet my family and he said yes. I was nervous about going back home.

We drove out to the country, to a large two-toned brown farmhouse and saw many cars in the driveway. Upon entering the house, I saw Dad, Aunt Art and my dad's girlfriend Sharon. I cannot remember who else was there but Aaron was welcomed with hugs, which he was not used to because his family was not the hugging type, or so he said. Aaron also met Tea Cup and she took right to him. She never took right to someone and by all the kisses she gave him, I felt sure that Aaron was the one for me. Dogs can usually sense things people cannot and I kept this in mind.

Breakfast went well with loads of food from eggs, pancakes, toast, coffee and so on. My family and Aaron grew to know more about each other and when Aaron and I left it was early afternoon. Aaron liked my family but I warned him that was only a small part of my family. He had not met my brothers and sisters.

I was glad breakfast had gone so well but I was still anxious. I was near my dad and still didn't know when his happy mood was going to go sour. I didn't want Eric to see that side of him. I'm glad we could get through breakfast and my dad's mood stayed a good one.

We spent the rest of the afternoon in my apartment and we never started his favorite dinner of Potato Salmon Pie until after seven. He worked on peeling, cutting and boiling potatoes while I worked on the pie crust.

We finished making dinner and spent a few more hours talking before Aaron had to leave for Vermont.

I never forgot how I felt that night and was very scared. I had had many moments where I felt like I was going to pass out but I had no idea why it was happening. I never even thought to say anything to my doctor, the fear of the incident caused me to push it out of my mind.

On May 31st, I had another appointment with my therapist. The conversation between my therapist and I went well and we are getting to know each other better. She was more understanding than my previous therapist. Anyway, my new therapist said that one of my doctors talked to said yes to having my dog, but that I really needed to talk to my doctor about it. Also, my therapist called DSS (Department of Social Services) and spoke with a woman about my Medicaid and the approval the dentist office said they needed. From my therapist, I heard that yes, the office does need the approval, but since I had not had any lapses in my Medicaid coverage I should be fine.

June 5-10, 2005, was an interesting feat for me. Aaron and I left for Vermont on June 5th and it was the first time I had ever been to Vermont. The drive lasted about four and a half hours, but that was nothing. Once I saw the Taconic and Green Mountain ranges, I was awestruck. I felt like I was in the middle of *The Lord of the Rings*. I told Aaron this. He smiled and said that where he lived in Arlington was referred to as the North Shire. I thought that was awesome he lived in the shire like the hobbits. Within my first few hours there, I could not help but wonder what it was like to live in Southern Vermont. Most of my stay was relaxing and Aaron and I just enjoyed our time together as well as seeing some of the sites and eating at local restaurants.

On the twelfth, I sadly had to leave Vermont and Aaron drove me home, back into loneliness, work, doctor's appointments, and the battle with my health, which have lessened while in Vermont. I knew the trouble with my health had not lessened, but my focus had shifted from me to Aaron and what we did together. In that sense, it seemed like I did not have as much trouble with my health.

On June 14th, I had an appointment with my therapist. My therapist also asked me if I asked my doctor, the one who checked my medications, about having my dog. I did not ask the one doctor because I thought I had to ask one of my *other* doctors about Tea Cup. I had so many doctors it became confusing. I had my primary care doctor, a dentist and then a therapist and a med management doctor for my psychiatric medications. I still hadn't yet accepted the fact I had a mental illness and what that could mean for my life. I continued to search for what else might be making me not feel well. I was certain it was my wisdom teeth. And unbeknownst to me at the time, gallbladder issues.

June 29th, I had an appointment at Mercy Behavioral Health to have my medications checked. I talked with my doctor about Zoloft and possibly taking me off it. Since I started taking it in late December, I had gained twenty-three pounds. This weight gain was what I had been working so hard to fight against.

The appointment went well. The dosages of Zoloft and Trazodone were lowered. Zoloft is now down to 100 mg and Trazodone is down to one pill at bedtime and only if I needed it. Both of these caused weight gain. My doctor left the Klonopin the same and said we should wait and see how I was doing after my surgery to see how I feel. If I did not need to be on the maintenance drugs than he would gradually take me off them. I could not stop taking them all at once as it would shock my nervous system and chemical balance in my body. At least that is how I understood it.

CHAPTER SEVEN

July 15th, I met with my therapist again and she noticed positive changes within me.

I told my therapist how much better I am feeling and she says that I look so much different. My eyes are brighter, I'm smiling, and she said she doesn't think she's ever heard me laugh before. I told her my plans of the future and couple of dreams that I have and that is to be the owner of a publishing company and of a recording studio. There is no way for me to do that unless I go to college and get a Business degree. So that is what I will look forward into doing. I will chat with Aaron about this later and see whether I should go to college here or there in Vermont. (I had decided I wanted to move in with Aaron.) As I was leaving, my therapist congratulated me on how I was doing and she said it would be great to see me be able to discontinue medication and therapy. I so can't wait for this to happen, Lord willing.

July 18th, I had a depressing day and started to doubt again if writing was what I wanted to do as a career. I was not sure what I wanted to do. I felt like there was a big void, like I should be doing something but I did not know what. Nothing seemed to spark my passion or so it seemed. I could not figure out if I had lost the desire to be a writer, or if I was so fatigued, the writing was too much effort.

July 25th, I had an appointment with my doctor in Clayton. I talked with him about possibly lowering my medication. I did not feel the drugs I was on were necessary after I had already been proven not to have depression. The anxiety I felt it was a result of my not feeling well and not understanding why. I did not always experience anxiety. Anxiety flared up during the moments I was not physically feeling well or had trouble breathing.

Zoloft was knocked down to fifty milligrams; Klonopin was down to a half tablet twice a day and both of these were taken at the new level for one week. The week after, Zoloft was taken every three days and Klonopin was down to a half tablet once a day. I estimated to be off the medications by August 8th. My decision to have my medications lowered and be weaned off them was not only due to the fact I did not believe I needed them, but also because I had made the decision to move to Vermont and live with Aaron. I wanted to be off the medications by the time I moved in late August.

July 28th marked my last day of therapy with my therapist. I told her I was feeling better about my life and was moving to Vermont with my boyfriend Aaron. She was happy to hear the good news and wished me well. That is also when she told me that my talk at the last session of going to college for business sparked in her the desire to go back to school and take a different career. Our last session was also her last day at that office. It felt good to positively influence someone.

I wrote a letter to TLS, Transitional Living Services, and gave them my thirty-day notice of when I would be leaving to move to Vermont. I could not wait to move, to get out of Watertown, a place that to me, felt void of creative outlets for me and housed too many memories and too much pain. I felt if I stayed, I would be trapped and would not be able to grow, to spread my wings as I have always dreamed. I did not want to be held back, nor did I want to continue to be near stressors that plagued me every day. By leaving the old behind, I would be able to start a new life.

August 5th, Aaron arrived and stayed the night with me and he slept on the couch. The following day he took me and my Chihuahua, Tea Cup, with him to Vermont for another vacation.

August 11th, we were still in Arlington, Vermont. I had a rough morning going through what I thought was Zoloft withdrawal. My body was numb, my head hurt almost constantly, though it was worse certain days. I was light-headed and very tired. My dreams were affected to a level of vividness so profound I sometimes had a hard time staying asleep because they were a little too real. I had body tremors but thought they were not as bad as they used to be.

Aaron's parents and brother were due to arrive and I wondered how I would feel when they arrived from Maine. I was so nervous and only hoped they would like me. By early evening, the folks arrived from Maine and they easily accepted me. We watched home videos, looked at pictures, and had a few drinks. The Maine accent his folks had shocked me. Aaron did not seem to have one, but then he had been living in Vermont for a few years. I was glad to meet his family, though I wondered if they would think any less of me if they knew how sick I was.

August 12th-14th, Aaron and I spent time with his family before they left for Maine on the fourteenth. They invited us to Thanksgiving Dinner. I was so excited! I could not wait for Thanksgiving to come so I could go to Maine to see where Aaron was from as well as to see Bangor and be so close to Stephen King's house. I would probably be inspired to write something.

August 19th, I dreaded the ride back to Watertown. I had knots of fear and uncertainty in my stomach. My heart missed home but my head was screaming, "No! I don't want to go back!" Nevertheless, I knew the return trip was inevitable. I tried to stay positive and remind myself that I would not be living in Watertown much longer. With that in mind, I knew I could stomach being home one more week.

August 20th, was the day of my dad's second marriage. He married a woman named Sharon who lived in Martinsburg, NY. I was generally having a good day until it came time to get ready for the wedding. Aaron was ready and my friend Kelly was going with us and she was ready. Everyone was waiting for me. I went through everything in my closet but could not find anything to wear. All of my clothes were too small and I cursed the antidepressants the doctors had me on. I had gained roughly thirty pounds after I had struggled years to lose all of that weight. I could not help but shed tears over this.

I found an outfit that fit, though not as well as I had liked. After I was calmed down and ready, we drove toward Martinsburg. We ended up missing a turn and therefore missed the wedding. We were able to make it to the reception and had a good time. On the other hand, I was exhausted and could not handle much of the celebration. I kept feeling like I should bolt from the situation. There was too much stimulation and so Aaron, Kelly, and I decided to leave early. I said good-bye to my dad and he cried, not wanting to release me from the hug. He knew that would be the last time he would see me before I moved to Vermont a few days later. I was sad in a way, but I was more than ready to leave and I felt I could not leave fast enough. I wanted to start a new, happier life with Aaron.

August 21st, Aaron went home. I was sad to see him leave but I knew I would be seeing him again in a few days. The twenty-second and twenty-third I spent packing my things. On the twenty-fifth, I went over to my sister Margie's for a farewell cookout for me. I also packed most of the day regardless of how exhausted and out of breath I was. No one else could pack for me and thus I had no choice but to push myself and finish the job.

On the twenty-sixth, I spent most of the day packing the rest of my stuff. Kelly and my brother Alex helped me move. Alex filled up his Buick and took some of my stuff to his place for storage and Kelly took some of my stuff to her place until I could pick it up. We piled the rest of my stuff into Aaron's Subaru Impreza. It was late, after midnight, when Aaron, Tea Cup, and I left for Vermont. Exhausted and stretched thin, I collapsed into the passenger seat and was silent most of the four and a half hours to Arlington, VT. I did think about how I was finally leaving my hometown and spreading my wings. No more feeling trapped and that my life was doomed to suffer stagnation.

The move to Vermont proved to be the best decision I had ever made. Life was difficult at first as I adjusted to the changes. My health still had not improved and I had no health insurance to continue seeing a doctor. That changed when Aaron and I were married on December 24, 2005. Now married, I was under Aaron's health insurance.

Early in 2006, I started seeing a doctor who discovered my body was overstimulated from fighting allergies and I was wheezing. She hit me hard with allergy and asthma medication until I could see an allergist. I often complained of trouble breathing but now I know it was from asthma.

When I saw an allergist, I went through skin prick tests that revealed several environmental allergies and food allergies. I had so many food allergies my husband and I sought out the advice of a nutritionist to guide me in getting enough nutrition from my new limited diet.

Seeing a nutritionist revealed I was gluten sensitive, severely malnourished to the point my cells were suffering, and I had adrenal fatigue.

Later, in September 2008, I started seeing a psychologist who tested for learning disabilities. My mother said I had a learning disability when I was younger, though we did not have a name for it. Thus, I decided to see someone who could help me discover more about this learning disability. After speaking with the psychologist, I learned I had anxiety issues, and signs of post-traumatic stress. Before the psychologist would test me for a learning disability, she decided I should see another woman in her office to help me handle anxiety and post-traumatic stress. Once, the latter two are taken care of, then she may decide to test me for my said learning disability.

Here we were back again at this mental illness crap. Why did this keep popping up? This couldn't be the real issue, couldn't it? I certainly didn't want it to be. I wanted it to be whatever physical thing was giving me issues, but then when you think about it, a chemical imbalance in the brain is a physical issue. I wasn't thinking of it this way. So I was back in therapy to talk about my dad and his treatment, and about the anxiety I have and what makes it worse.

I continued to have ups and downs to the point my life was so affected by this emotional roller coaster. I was struggling. But then again my doctor said I had allergies and they were overstimulating my body. So maybe that was it instead. Allergies and asthma are what I focused on next and not a mental illness. I kept throwing mental illness out the window.

CHAPTER EIGHT

ECT & Ketamine Treatment

Lately, I have been going through teletherapy where I talk to a therapist through my computer. We talk about all things that might be causing my anxiety or working with and changing my negative thoughts using CBT, cognitive behavioral therapy.

I didn't talk much about therapy in my story but I went. I went to a therapist while we were in Vermont. I went to five therapists here in Maine. It's hard to find a therapist you click with, but I think I have done that this last time.

I also haven't talked much about my stay at Acadia Hospital. The last time I stayed was over a year ago and that's a milestone for me. I have never been stable for that long and the ketamines I know are a big part of that.

After about a month of IOP groups came ECT, or shock therapy. I passed by the ECT wing every day of IOP groups and I remember thinking "I'm glad I don't have to go down there." How quickly the situation changed. I walked into the waiting room and was called in a little while later. I was taken into the prep room where they put the IV in and take your vitals. Once the IV is in, I used the restroom and then walked into the ECT room. I laid down on the gurney and there were three or four nurses around me and the doctor was at the end of the bed near a computer.

One nurse told me she was going to give me something to counteract the Klonopin I was on. Boy, when she did that I was super anxious and emotional. I did not do well and became scared. Shortly after that, I was off to sleep. Then I woke up in the recovery room. I did well for my first few treatments. Things went better when I told them about the med that counteracts the Klonopin made me super anxious and then they started giving it to me after I was asleep. So that went much better for me and I wasn't afraid of ECT. It's not like they make it out in the movies. I was thanking God that it wasn't like that.

Basically, after your asleep, they emit a small amount of energy that comes through this headband like contraption and you have small seizures. Sometimes they are one-sided other times they are bilateral, or two-sided. They did the bilateral on me.

I did start to notice I was feeling better, but unfortunately, I had to stop the ECT because I was losing my short term memory.

It was after ECT that I was asked if I wanted to try ketamine infusions. I was feeling miserable and I sat there in the doctor's office not having a clue what these infusions were. I realized I didn't care. I was so depressed I was thinking of suicide and cutting myself and I didn't like the emotional or mental space I was in. I thought of my kids and husband and realized I had nothing to lose. I was already at rock bottom. I couldn't get any lower.

I looked at the doctor who stared back at me with blue eyes looking through a pair of rims and she was tall, thin with short brown hair. "Yes. I'll do it," I said with a sigh.

"Okay. We'll get you scheduled on your way out."

As I walked toward the Exit I stopped at the window and got my appointments from the lady behind the desk. There were four dates, which surprised me, but okay so I had to come in four times for this treatment.

No one could have prepared me for what I was going to experience the day the first infusion came. I walked into the hospital and made my way to the ECT wing where I checked in at the window. I waited until I was called back. The first thing I had to do was pee in a cup for drug screening. I would have to do this each time I came in for the infusions.

After the drug test, I was taken back into the recovery room where they usually put ECT patients. There is room for three hospital beds and the third one is for a person going through a ketamine infusion. That bed was mine.

I laid down and waited for the nurse to get the IV lead into my arm because that's how the ketamines were given. I'm a challenging stick so it was interesting each time I went in to see how long it would take the nurse to get the IV ready. Sometimes this was the longest part of the appointment.

So once I was set, and we had to wait for the doctor to finish with an ECT treatment, I answered a series of questions that would determine my depression score. Sixty was the high and my score was in the mid-thirties which is depressed.

I looked at the nurse and I was curious about this whole ketamine thing. "So what are ketamines anyway?"

"Well, ketamines used to be given with anesthesia before people went into surgery and they noticed the patients would always say they felt better afterward. They realized it was the ketamines. I do have to warn you though some people have hallucinations. They see family members at the end of their bed and see really weird stuff. You might have some strange sensations."

Oh, great! Exactly what I wanted to hear.

Soon after the doctor arrived at my bedside. "Are you to do this, Janis?"

"Yes."

"Okay." She looked at the nurse beside her.

"Are we ready for Time Out?"

"Yes, we are," said the nurse.

What? Time out? Are they putting me to sleep? I thought nervously.

"We are ready to start the infusion. Do you give us permission, Janis?" The doctor looked down at me waiting for an answer.

"Yes," I said my heart now racing, pounding so hard I could feel it in my chest. My body tightened with anxiety. *What was going to happen? What's this stuff going to do? How is it going to make me feel? Am I going to be okay?* My mind was racing with all of these thoughts over and over.

The doctor started the ketamine infusion and I laid there watching the ceiling and occasionally looking around. *Is something supposed to happen because nothing's happening.* I waited longer and the things I was hearing around me started to sound distorted almost far away like. Then I moved my hand back and forth in front of my face and was so marveled at the multiple hands I saw. My body went numb. I couldn't tell if I was breathing and this made me anxious. I prayed to God that He was watching over me and that He would keep me breathing. Also, when I would talk to the nurse to let her know how I was doing I could hear myself talking but I couldn't feel it. If this is what tripping out was like I don't know how people do it. I didn't like not having control over what was happening to me.

The infusion lasted about forty-five minutes and then they waited about an hour before allowing me to sit up and then walk to the waiting room. I did okay. I was a little wobbly walking but not bad. I made it out to the front of the building where I got my ride home.

I went through the next three treatments. The second treatment was similar to the first only I knew what to expect and my anxiety didn't get as bad. The third and fourth treatments were easier. I knew what to expect because the distortions and hallucinations were always the same. These last two times, the hallucinations had actually calmed down and I didn't have multiple hands moving in front of my face. It was just my one hand. I not only noticed that the hallucinations were less powerful, I did notice, like the people before me, I felt so much better.

After my last treatment I had to answer the questions I answered at the beginning to see where my depression level was. It had dropped from mid-thirties to zero. I felt great and had a ton of energy. I was enjoying life, enjoying my family and kids, taking care of the house, cleaning, just doing everything I was too depressed to do before.

I had prayed for years that God would lead me and the doctors to something that would help me in treating my depression. I had been trying one medication after another since 2004 and that was back when I lived in my hometown of Watertown, New York. Since then I had moved to Vermont in 2005 when I met my husband online, and then in 2011 he got a job in his home state of Maine so we moved with our daughter there.

In all three states I had been through different treatments, therapy, hospitalizations in New York and Maine. Nothing seemed to work very well. Of course, it didn't help at the beginning I was given antidepressants when I was bipolar only the bipolar piece we didn't know until I was diagnosed in May of 2017. The antidepressants made me worse.

Now the ketmaines help so well. I do great for about two to three weeks but then have a steady downfall. I thought I could go right back in when I started feeling depressed again. I was so scared to go back to rock bottom when I was having suicidal thoughts and hurting myself. I didn't want to go back to that dark place. I was so scared. I was even more scared when I was told that the hospital was only allowed to give the ketamine treatment every three months. So I had to wait.

November 6th, 2017 was my last treatment. And I have been going down hill for a couple of months. I was just hospitalized at the end of December because I started to have thoughts of harming my kids and some thoughts of hurting myself and I couldn't promise that I'd be safe if I went home. I was tearful every day and had a hard time not crying throughout the day. I was also highly irritable and I would get so angry for no reason. I so hate having issues with my mood. I hate that my kids and husband have to see it. It tears at me inside, breaks my heart. But I have learned not to feel guilty about.

For the longest time I felt guilt, but my husband kept telling me that mood disorders run in my family and so does depression. That I was dealing with a genetic issue and that I was getting help and doing everything I could to get the help I needed. And it dawned on me. I was doing everything I knew how to do to get help and I had to remember to use my coping skills, and to pray and spend time with God. So often I prayed to God and just blurted everything out to Him. I knew He would listen and out of anyone I talked to He would be the best one to understand what I was going through. So I talked to God and I cried my little heart out. I entrusted my very life to Him and rested in His care.

So many times when I feel emotional I go and lay down, take a few deep breaths and imagine I am resting curled up in God's loving hands and I usually fall asleep.

Not having any guilt for what I have to deal with helps lift some of the burden I'd feel and I wouldn't feel bad for having to go off in another room away from the family and deal with my emotions. It was a lot better than taking irritability and anger out on them.

I also use meditation apps on my iPad from Glenn Harold. He has a wonderful voice and I love his accent. Just following his suggestions help relieve anxiety and also help me to be mindful of the moment I'm in to get the most of it. Now you don't have to go and buy Glenn's mediation apps. He might be a place to start, but you can certainly try out other apps. I just really like Glenn's work.

Anyway. Come Monday, January 15th, 2018, I made another trip to Acadia Hospital which is the mental health hospital around here in Bangor, Maine. I went under another ketamine infusion at 8AM. I had another infusion on the 17th. This round instead of doing four treatments and then stopping they did six treatments. Two one week, wait two weeks, have another treatment, wait two weeks and so on until six treatments were finished. Then I had two weeks where I waited and then came back in for a follow up to see how I was doing.

I was feeling pretty depressed and I answered questions like I usually do when I go in, which gives them my depression score. I was in the 30s which wasn't good. I explained to the doctor I have just been in this depressive phase of sleeping all of the time, low energy and no interest to do anything. But I told her it was a phase and I knew I would come out of it after about a week to two weeks. It was just a matter of waiting it out. I knew I'd pop back up into hypomania. The doctor didn't like how I was cycling so fast and she said that must be a miserable way to live. Truth is, I have been getting used to it. It's just gone on that long. So she asked me about trying lithium because it's supposed to be really good at leveling out the ups and downs of bipolar. I told her I was willing to try it. So currently that is what I am on and after about a week I have to have my blood tested to check the lithium levels in my blood and to check for thyroid function because lithium likes to mess up the thyroid. So that takes me up to the present. The lithium is helping me to feel better in just a few days time. I don't feel so emotional all the time but also something I have to remember is I'm in my hypomanic stage so I generally feel good during this stage anyway. I'm beginning to wonder where the "normal" is in all of this. Where is my "normal" side. I'm either too low or hypomanic.

So far the ketamine injections that are supposed to be happing this month may not be happening at all. The doctor who does the injections wants my lithium levels in the therapeutic range. So my does has been increased twice and I have to go back and have labs done again. And this is not the only thing going on. I got a phone call from the ECT department where they do the ketamine infusions as well, I was told that they are low on staff members and can barely do ECT treatments. So for right now there is no one to do the ketamine infusions. This is as of May 24, 2018.

On the end of October 2018 after my last infusion I went hypomanic. The lithium I went on had to be increased several times before I could have another ketamine infusion, which wasn't going to happen soon. I only had two treatments in October down form my six. This is because a new hospital policy was in place of only being able to have twelve treatments in a year. I had had fifteen. So the next time I could start treatments again was after February nineteenth.

The doctor is working with someone out west who runs a ketamine clinic and her policy is that if you need treatment you get it. The doctor I see is trying to adopt that policy.

In early 2019, I wasn't able to get ketamine infusions anymore because there weren't enough doctors or nurses to do the job. About a year later I got a call asking if I still needed ketamine infusion but I told the receptionist that I had been stable without it and that I didn't think I needed them anymore. And to this date, February 19, 2020, Wednesday, I am still stable just on the lithium and vraylar. Other than that I am on in teletherapy a couple of times a month, but the appointments change as I need them too.

CHAPTER NINE

Looking Back

I, Janis I. Soucie, admit that I have mental illnesses that require medications and ketamine infusions to treat. Mental Illnesses are nothing to be ashamed of. My brain thinks in different ways and the chemical imbalances need help. There is no treatment that works one hundred percent so I'll still have my ups and downs, but hopefully, they won't be too bad. I am still working on not feeling guilty for having this illness. It's an illness that would be treated like another illness. Say you had cancer. You would treat that, by using different methods. And no matter what treatment you go through you need a support system. For mental illness, I think it is needed more so because the illness is invisible and when people can't see that your physically handicapped they assume you're okay. That's not true. Mental Illness gives off many signs. Sometimes you have to look for them, but my husband is so good at telling me when I'm depressed before I even am aware of it myself.

When you have a mental illness, a support system is key. You need people you can talk to that won't judge you and who won't just throw you away because you're no fun anymore, and you don't need someone telling you you're fine, because you know you're not, that person doesn't believe you. You need people who will believe you and help you however they can because living with a mental illness and emotional instability just plain sucks! You're miserable all the time. Do people just think you want to live this way? No way! It's not a choice. It was how we were born for some of us. For others, it may have been a traumatic event. But we didn't choose this kind of life, but I know we can fight it. We can do the very best we can to lead awesome lives!

Okay, now that I'm done with my rant.

But going through everything I've gone through and looking back on it all helps me open my eyes to what was going on in my childhood with my dad. There were signs I could tell he was in a good mood and when he was in a bad mood. And my dad slept a lot too. Could that have been a sign of depression?

Everything I have been experiencing are things I noticed my dad was also experiencing. So could his mood swings have been caused by mental illness and I just got it from him? There are several people in my family who deal with depression, anxiety, suicidal ideation and there has been one attempt, luckily my sister survived.

But I'm seeing my dad in a different light because of my mental illness when in my childhood, just undiagnosed, and I know this caused me to see his illness in a different perhaps more scary way. You see I was already dealing with anxiety issues as a kid so I was afraid a lot. My brother was concerned, and my dad even asked me if I wanted to go talk to someone, I wanted to go, but I said "no" out of fear. Also, going to "talk to someone" was something that always seemed looked down upon and I didn't want that. I didn't want people to look down on me.

Seeing that my dad more than likely had a mental illness I felt sad for him for what he was going through silently. He could have gotten help and had a better life and made better relationships with his wife and children than what he had. Family life could have been so much better. But in that generation, you don't talk about things like that. I don't like how things happened, but I do know that God takes negative things and uses them to mold us into His son's character and to make us a better person than what we currently are. There is always room for improvement. No one is perfect. God can take what you feel and what you're going through and change things

for the better in your life. You may not see the results right away, or even while you walk this Earth, but you will see the Potter making changes in you, His beloved child. He will never forget you or what you're going through. You are etched in his heart forever. He loves you and always will.

About the Author

Janis I. Soucie (Monroe is her maiden name) is an article, novel writer and poet. Her articles have been published in the National Health Federation Magazine and website. Her poetry has appeared in several chapbooks by the J.M.W. Publishing Company and has also appeared in a Vermont magazine, EverChanging, and a U.K. magazine, Poetic Hours. When she's not writing, you can find her in the kitchen, singing at the top of her lungs while she bakes goodies to her heart's delight. You can visit her at jisoucie.com.

Connect with Janis

Amazon: https://www.amazon.com/-/e/B07B9GLT8P
Facebook: https://www.facebook.com/jisoucie/
Pinterest: https://www.pinterest.com/jisoucie/
LinkedIn: https://www.linkedin.com/in/jisoucie/
Blog: http://jisoucie.com

Published Books

A Breeze of Whispers (a compilation poetry book)
Reflections of the Heart: A Memoir
The History of Sackets Harbor, New York

Author's Note

In Watertown, New York is where the events for this book
started taking place and in Glenburn, Maine is where I still continue
to get treatment for bipolar II, anxiety, and PTSD. At the time of
writing this book, I am continuing not only with medications.

www.ingramcontent.com/pod-product-compliance
Lightning Source LLC
Chambersburg PA
CBHW032028040426
42448CB00006B/767